Sugar's Journey Home

Written by Stacy Snyder • Illustrated by Anne Johnson

Sugar's Journey Home. Second Edition. Ages 3-9.

Text copyright ©2021 by Stacy Snyder. Illustration copyright ©2022 by Anne Johnson.
For information please contact anne@wagdesign.be or stacysnyder@mac.com

First edition: USA 2022 ISBN: 978-0-9600041-7-1

This book is based on the true story
of two rescue animals who found each other
and became Best Friends.

Charger, the dog, had made it home after a long journey.
She had left me behind with Sticker and Henry.

The Lady in the Red Hat was in her garden.
She was upset that Charger and I were gone.
Her head was in her hands
and tears were running down her face.
She did not see Charger.

Suddenly,
she felt something on her cheek.

As she raised her head,
there was Charger,
licking away her tears.

The Lady in the Red Hat grabbed Charger and hugged her.

"Charger! Where have you been? I have been so worried about you. Where is Sugar?" she asked. Charger whined in distress.

"Okay, Charger, we will wait for her. I'm so happy you are home!"

Meanwhile, I was on the other side of the forest where I found my parents locked up in an old shed. I paced anxiously—

— trying to decide when to set them free.

Sticker said, "Don't you think we should wait
and ask the Moon and Sparkle when to go?"

I impatiently replied,

"No, Sticker!
We need to leave NOW!"

8

I opened the door
to the shed with my nose.

"Come on, Mom and Dad.
We need to leave."

We all headed out across a large, green, field.

All of a sudden,
a tractor was driving quickly towards us.

The tractor stopped right in our path
and out stepped the Farmer.

2B – KIND

"Hey! Where do you think you are going?"
I was surprised. Standing in front of us
was the Farmer who had made me haul
his heavy wood.

2B-KIN

"AH, HA!" he said. "I remember you!
Now, I have three horses to haul my wood."

I cried out to Henry the Hawk,
         "Henry, please, help us!"

Peck!

Peck!

Peck!

Peck!

Peck!

Peck!

Peck!

Henry,
please help us!

Henry swooped down
and started pecking
at the Farmer's hat, —

— but the Farmer still
caught me and my parents!

14

He tied us to his tractor
and took us back to the old shed.

15

I hung my head.
I felt bad for not being patient.

"I am so sorry, Sticker!
We must wait for the Moon and Sparkle
to appear tonight and ask them what to do."

If only Sugar
had listened!

16

"That night the Moon and Sparkle shone brightly down.
—They told me and my parents not to frown.

Be patient, we will show you the way.
—You will all be home in one more day."

Sticker was hiding in the tall grass
listening to the Moon and Sparkle.

The Moon said,
  "Tonight you will see a ring around me,
    which means there will be a light rain.

In the morning,
    the Sun will rise and welcome you with a beautiful Rainbow.
      Follow the Rainbow to the giant tree,
        and there you will find *your* 'pot of gold' …HOME!"

19

BEST FRIENDS!

LOVE♡

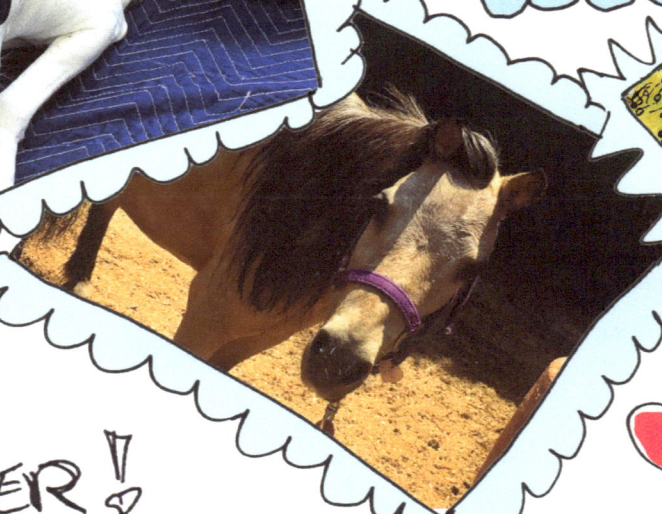

FOREVER!

GOOD TIMES

Now go back and see if you can spot any of these friendly little creatures.

Dragonfly

Horseshoe

Woodpecker

Owl

Possum

Calico cat

Follow us in our next book,

Home Around the Campfire.

STACY SNYDER is a graduate of the University of Arizona, with a degree in Special Education. She resides in San Diego California, with her loving husband John. She is the mother of two daughters, and the grandmother of four beautiful grandchildren. Her background in education and love for nature were the inspiration for this book. She was taken by the extraordinary relationship that developed between a rescued dog and a rescued miniature horse. Their unconditional love is a heart-warming example of kindness.

ANNE JOHNSON has held a career in painting, illustration and fine arts for over 30 years. She received a Bachelor of Arts degree from Roanoke College followed by a Master of Arts degree in Medical Illustration from the Medical College of Georgia, now Georgia Health Sciences University. She has an endless love for animals and nature and has been passionate about children's books since she was a young girl. After residing in Belgium for over 25 years she has recently returned to her hometown, Wayzata, Minnesota, and is the proud mother of three loving young adults, two dogs, a cat, and a horse. *Sugar's Journey Home* is her third book with Stacy Snyder.

SUGAR is a rescued buckskin miniature horse. She was in very poor shape when she was adopted. Scared and very skittish. With patience and spending lots of time with her, she has become a loving, contented horse with the help of her friend Charger. Age unknown.

CHARGER was adopted as a puppy, and has grown into a large, strong dog with a very happy disposition. Charger loved to go on walks with her best friend Sugar on a double leash. She also insisted on wearing sunglasses. Charger passed away peacefully in 2021 at the age of 12.

This sequel is dedicated to
the beautiful children, grand-children, cousins, nieces and nephews
that have all played an important part in its development.

Thanks to the loving support of this close-knit family
and the special bond between the author and the artist,
this book series is able to continue.

*We would like to give special thanks to
the wonderful librarians of the Rancho Santa Fe Library
for their invaluable time, meticulous input and endless support.*

Use these blank pages to draw any of your favorite characters.

www.ingramcontent.com/pod-product-compliance
Lightning Source LLC
Chambersburg PA
CBHW040712150426

42811CB00061B/1857